Jesus Is My Friend!

Written by Josep Codina
Illustrated by Roser Rius

PRAYING WITH LITTLE ONES

Pauline
BOOKS & MEDIA

Jesus, you were once little like me.
You also enjoyed playing with your
friends.

Jesus, your parents Mary
and Joseph loved you a lot.
They taught you
to work, to pray, to love....

Jesus, when you grew up,
you loved little children.

THANK YOU FOR LOVING ME, TOO!

Jesus, many people came
to hear you speak about our
Heavenly Father.

Jesus, four of your friends wrote down
many things that you said and did.
The book they wrote is called the Gospel.
These friends traveled all over the world
to tell people about you.

Jesus, the people loved you because you were very good. You helped everyone who needed help.
You loved sick people and poor people in a special way.

Jesus, some people didn't
like some things you said
and did. They got very angry.
They made you die
on a cross.
But you forgave the people
who hurt you. You kept on
loving them. We remember
your love with the sign
of the cross. Help us to love
everyone as you did—
even when it's hard.

Jesus, you are God.
After you died,
you came back
to life again! Then you
went to heaven to
prepare a place for all
your friends in God
our Father's house.
We will all live with you
there someday!

To Parents and Teachers

If we want children to open their hearts to Jesus, and this must always be the reference point of the Christian life, we have to introduce Jesus to them in a way that rouses both their admiration and their confidence. The Jesus whom we initially present to children must be the Jesus of the Gospel. Having encountered him through God's Word, children will gradually come to know him more deeply through further religious instruction and the experiences of life.

This little book helps children to reflect on some aspects of Jesus' life. The illustrations can provide a springboard for your added age-appropriate explanations of Jesus' words and actions.

Jesus, when you grew up,
you loved little children.

THANK YOU FOR LOVING ME, TOO!

Pauline Books and Media Centers operated by the Daughters of St. Paul:

3908 Sepulveda Blvd., Culver City, CA 90230   310-397-8676

5945 Balboa Ave., San Diego, CA 92111   858-565-9181

46 Geary St., San Francisco, CA 94108   415-781-5180

145 SW 107th Ave., Miami, FL 33174   305-559-6715

1143 Bishop St., Honolulu, HI 96813   808-521-2731

For Neighbor Islands: 800-259-8463

172 N. Michigan Ave., Chicago, IL 60601   312-346-4228

4403 Veterans Blvd., Metairie, LA 70006   504-887-7631

Rt 1, 885 Providence Hwy., Dedham, MA 02026   781-326-5385

9804 Watson Rd., St. Louis, MO 63126   314-965-3512

561 US Rt. 1, Wick Plaza, Edison, NJ 08817   732-572-1200

150 E. 52nd St., New York, NY 10022   212-754-1110

2105 Ontario St., Cleveland, OH 44115   216-621-9427

9171-A Roosevelt Blvd., Philadelphia, PA 19114   215-676-9494

243 King St., Charleston, SC 29401   843-577-0175

4811 Poplar Ave., Memphis, TN 38117   901-761-2987

114 Main Plaza, San Antonio, TX 78205   210-224-8101

1025 King St., Alexandria, VA 22314   703-549-3806

3022 Dufferin St., Toronto, Ontario, Canada M6B 3T5   416-781-9131

1155 Yonge St., Toronto, Ontario, Canada M4T 1W2   416-934-3440

Original title: *Vull ser el teu amic!*

English adaptation by Patricia Edward Jablonski, FSP

Copyright © 2002, Editorial Claret, S.A.
Barcelona, Spain (World Rights)

ISBN 0-8198-3974-4

Published in the U.S.A. by Pauline Books & Media,
50 Saint Pauls Avenue, Boston, MA 02130-3491.

Printed in Spain.

www.pauline.org

Pauline Books & Media is the publishing house of
the Daughters of St. Paul, an international congregation
of women religious serving the Church with the communications media.

1 2 3 4 5   06 05 04 03 02